The Other Side Of Through

Rosemary Hill

Pearly Gates Publishing, LLC, Houston, Texas

The Other Side Of Through

The Other Side of Through

Copyright © 2018
Rosemary Hill

All Rights Reserved.
No portion of this publication may be reproduced, stored in any electronic system, or transmitted in any form or by any means (electronic, mechanical, photocopy, recording, or otherwise) without written permission from the author or publisher.
Brief quotations may be used in literary reviews.

ISBN 13: 978-1-947445-06-2
Library of Congress Control Number: 2018932401

Scripture references used with permission from Zondervan via Biblegateway.com.
Public Domain.

For information and bulk ordering, contact:
Pearly Gates Publishing, LLC
Angela R. Edwards, CEO
P.O. Box 62287
Houston, TX 77205
BestSeller@PearlyGatesPublishing.com

DEDICATION

I dedicate this book to a few people who were instrumental in my journey to wholeness and wellness—emotionally, mentally, and physically:

Ashely D. Hill, Amber D. Hill, and David A. Hill, Jr.: To my kids —you were there for me much of my journey. Some of it is your journey as well. There are things not mentioned in this book because I was not led to share them—mostly because of you. I am unaware of just how deeply my journey impacted you, and I want the three of you to know that although I made some good decisions, I also made some bad ones. They were all made with the very best intentions. I would like to believe that not leaving the marriage sooner was in your best interest. I must admit: It really was because I did not know my own strength. As I reflect on my journey, I see a woman who was afraid of so many things, and the biggest was being 'flawed'. I pray that you learn it's okay to be flawed; it's okay to let go; and it's okay to not just start over, but get right back up, take your fighting stance, or simply move your feet until you are no longer in an unsafe place — or until you have reached the other side. I thank you for the love, support, and respect you have always shown towards me as your mother, as your Sister-in-Christ, and as your friend. This book is dedicated to you in hopes that you, too, will find strength and encouragement. Take note of where you are in your journey. It is important to know when you're entering a storm, when you are in the midst of the storm, and when you have made it to the other side of the storm. I apologize for the times you carried me. My job as a parent is to carry you and lift you up, and although there may be a day when you may have to care for me, that time is not now. For what you have already done, thank you. I pray God blesses each of you for being a blessing to me! Thank you for the wonderful welcome home from the hospital and the sticky notes all over my mirror. They still give me goosebumps as I read them from time to time to remind me: We have the VICTORY in Jesus!

Norma Shaw: My Momma—I found a strength deep inside me that once I tapped into it, I looked in the mirror and saw YOU. Mom, I am sorry this journey became so heavy for me. I am sorry I lost my way, my will, and my fight. I watched you shoulder so much pain, hurt, death, and disappointment—then, you balled it up and threw it back at the world. You told your paid that if it was going to stick around, it could only sit in the corner and be quiet. You silenced the enemy when he came charging at you. I so wanted to be like you. I wanted my children to see me as I see you, and I lost it. I tried to carry it all, but when I fell, you were right there to help me up. I thank you that as I traveled to the other side of through, you kept me close. I heard your prayers, Momma, when you asked God to send

His angels. He heard you. He sent them, and they helped me to the other side of through. My journey is not over but that season is over, and I am never to pass through that way again. I love you, Mom.

Tommie L. Shaw: My Father—Thank you for all you did to help raise me to be the person I am. I learned the true meaning of helping people as I watched you fix cars, help someone find a home, or even give someone a home. You supported me in high school and was my biggest fan when Shennetta and I ran track relays. I loved hearing your version of how well our relay team did because they were so animated and made me smile. You would tell me that without us, they didn't have a track team. I knew better though; it took all four of us to finish the race. May you rest in peace, knowing that all you taught me was useful on my journey.

Dr. Judy Jacobs: Thank you for the counseling you provided me during the hardest and darkest moments of my life. Counseling is necessary, and I am forever grateful you took care of my children and me by helping us to heal emotionally. You reminded us how much God loves us and of the power we possess through Him to overcome the challenges and tragic losses we experience. The marriage could not be saved, but you saved my life by helping me decide to take the journey to the other side. I am forever grateful for the sessions and phone calls.

Kisha Kyler: I thank you for always praying for my family and me. I appreciate the phone calls, texts, and always letting me know you are proud of me. You are an amazing Woman of God, and I'm extremely proud of you and Chris.

Amber Alexander: Thank you for loving me as your friend. Thank you for running the Army

Ten-Miler with me. I still can't believe what an amazing runner you are! You refused to leave me behind (even though you could have finished at least a half-hour before me and my bad knees), you stayed with me, and, more importantly, you finished with me. Amber, this is indicative of how you stayed with me and prayed with and for me during this journey. I look back on this journey and smile at God's Word when it tells us, "He will never leave us nor forsake us" (Deuteronomy 31:6). Your loving spirit reflects God's love, kindness, and tender mercy. You are so many things to so many people, but to me, you are an amazing friend.

Seble Bynum: The conversations we have are funny, they are honest, and they are free-flowing. The thing that makes our conversations amazing is that they are REAL. I love that when we talk, no matter how long it has been, we connect — with the most important things to us both are that we are okay and that our families are okay. I am grateful for you. You expressed much empathy after learning I had gone through so much on this journey, and you almost felt as though you let me down. Seble, you were exactly where you were supposed to be, and I thank you for that.

Francis and Lisa Hayden: I am simply blown away by how both of you took time from your lives to love my family and me. Lisa, you were there for quite a bit of my storm. There were times I would not share all I was going through because it was not time; however, with your discernment, I am sure you knew, and you just prayed for me. You quickly learned who I was and trusted me to be your friend and part of your family. The countless conversations and emotions that you and I have shared helped me get through some tough situations. Whether we were talking about how good God is, His amazing love for us, or in tears laughing about how messed up shipments were in the warehouse, you were and still are my friend and my sister. I love you both and thank you for continuing to be there for me.

Pastor Jeffery Smith and Lady Nicola Smith: My spiritual parents who, every Sunday and Wednesday, bring forth love, wisdom, intellect, and shows compassion for every member of Strong Tower Ministries in Fredericksburg, Virginia. When my husband left me, Lady Nicola, you did not leave my side. You called and texted me to make sure I was doing well. You prayed with me, and you prayed for my children and me that God would cover us. Thank you for creating an environment of love at Strong Tower Ministries, and for reminding me of the importance of telling my story.

Rene Hill: You were never my "Sister-in-Law" because the day we met, you were my friend — and then quickly became my big sister. During my journey, you called and sent cards and flowers, but it was your prayers that got me through. I thank you for sharing your journey with me, as it helped me to understand that I was not the first or last person to have their spouse of over 20 years leave them. It was funny how when you would go to your therapy appointments, you would come back and share with me what you learned. I get teary-eyed as I think of the strength it must have taken to seek help and understanding for yourself, and still save a little to give to me. Your love shown towards me was unselfish, and I thank you for everything you did to support me along the way.

Carmella Smith: My Bestie—There are so many things I can say to you, but this dedication is to share with the world how you have been there for me during my journey to the other side of through. It has been difficult. Each time I started to write my 'thank you', I found myself talking about how much fun we had in high school or recalling some of the challenges we faced. During this journey, it was confirmed that God placed you in my life for a season, a reason, and a lifetime because just like always, I did not have to tell you how I was feeling: you just knew. It was like I was hurting so bad, you felt my pain. It was evident because each word you spoke to me was exactly what I needed to hear at the exact time I needed to hear it. With all that you had going on with your family, you made time for me...your best friend. Thank you for over 30 years of friendship and for joining me on this journey from across the miles as I now share my story with the world.

Ingrid Williams: Affectionately known as "My MeMe"—I thank you for being a friend and a sister to me. I appreciate your genuine support and am forever grateful for your mentorship and guidance in becoming a part of the best sorority on the planet. Your faith and trust in me as a

Contracting Professional means the world to me, and I am honored you engage in the fun conversations with me about the Federal Acquisition Regulation (FAR). You know that's a love story, right? During my journey, you always took time to listen and just sit on the phone with me. You would ask me questions, and unbeknownst to you, you were helping me think through things. You helped me get through the task at hand — one step at a time and one task at a time as I moved closer to the other side of through. Thank you!

Dr. Brenda T. Bradley: I am not making mention of you in this book because you introduced me to **Angela Edwards** at Pearly Gates Publishing. Nor am I mentioning you because you allowed me to co-author a book you published entitled *I Feel Good* which, in fact, became an International Best-Selling Book. And it is surely not because you are the mastermind behind the '21-Day Vegan

Challenge' (which I completed TWICE). The mention is simply because you have a heart for people. As I watch you, I love to see that your journey is not about you; it's about others. You are gorgeous and down to earth, with simplicity and class. You love and laugh on purpose and with purpose! I do want to publicly thank you for introducing me to Angela Edwards, for her Christian publishing house is what I needed at this part of my journey to share my testimony I had been holding onto. You were there for me when I had to revisit the emotions and feelings while going "through". You listened to my story with compassion and amazement, recognizing the sensitivity of the topic and providing me with advice I needed to hear that gave me strength to unpack from my journey. Thank you for it all!

Jarvis B. Bradley: You support all those around you with ease and challenge us all to be GREAT! You are a great conversationalist, and I appreciate your eclectic taste in all things. In some way, each day you share your energy with others so that your light might send a spark to flame someone else's torch. You take delight in not only seeing others succeed, but you are always willing to help. I ask God to bless you and your family for being a blessing to me and giving me your gift of friendship. I know that sometimes, your journey may get tiring, but I pray your strength and that God will refill your cup for being a good person. I met you at a stage in this journey when I was broken, and you made me laugh. For that moment, you forced me to forget about the journey. You demanded I just breathe and enjoy the moment. My eyes were opened. I am now "woke". I pray my laughter, hunger for success, and desire to see others succeed are as contagious as yours. My hopes are that all you extended to me, I will extend to others as I share my journey. Stay focused, Jarvis. I pray your success, as well as that of your family. Lastly, thank you for introducing me to your "twin", Dr. Brenda T. Bradley.

Melvin Harrison: You have been more than a brother; you have been an amazing friend to me. Our conversations are always on FIRE! When we talk about the Word of God and what He has done in our lives, we get so excited and have our own little preaching-party. Thank you for praying for me and speaking new beginnings into my life. You always let me know you are proud of me and always hearing my heart. There were many times during my journey that you spoke directly to my situation without even knowing. I am grateful because sometimes, life can hurt so much, I am unsure I could put the words together to tell you how I was feeling. Thank you.

Narrissia Harrison: During this journey, I did not share many things with you because I did not know how. I still think about why I never called you when I was falling apart, especially when this journey got to be too much for me. As my big sister, I believe the ways in which you were there for me growing up helped to prepare me for this journey. You showed me how to use my support systems around me. Long before I tossed the word "networking" around as an adult, you had already shown me how to negotiate, network, and make things happen. You were the reason I went into the military, and the same strength and confidence I saw in you is the same strength and confidence I knew I needed to get to the other side of through. Thank you for showing me the ropes.

Rose Mae Smith: Although your life was cut way too short, you, my beautiful Aunt, influenced my journey many years back with the way you sought to learn a little about everything. I really wish I could have shared this story with you because I am sure you had something you would have told me that would have reached even more people. This thing I call 'the other side of through' may have been a drop in the bucket for you, as I am sure you had many journeys that (sadly) will never be shared. The dark moments I know you had, I pray are strongly reflected in this story so that light will be shed and expose all that may have kept you bound. I do not know firsthand of any specific journey you may have taken; however, I do know that you were a woman of class, dignity, intellect, and many talents. Those things combined always make the enemy tremble. Rest in peace, my beautiful Aunt. Rest in peace.

Others I would like to thank are (in no particular order): **Aaron Harrison, Brandon Shaw, Cassandra Cooks, Yee Hang, Kimberly Morgan, Zelica Johnson, Stacy Smith, Megan Hill-Bonner, Richard Alves, George Antoniou, Joy Champion, Deloris Brown, Marcia Leftwich, Ceresh Perry, Erika Dawson, Christopher and**

Latrice Holmes, Trena Mitchell, Sharon Mulvey, Christine Sordillo, Maribel Vasquez, and **Sylvia Walker.**

To my family and friends not mentioned specifically: Thank you for continuing to support me, both personally and professionally.

"May the God of hope fill you with all joy and peace as you trust in Him, so that you may overflow with hope by the power of the Holy Spirit" (Romans 15:13, NIV).

Rosemary Hill

PREFACE

*"Lord, as I begin my journey to the other side of through, I pray you order my steps. You said in your Word, **"The steps of a good man are ordered by the Lord"** (Psalm 37:23). Lord, sometimes I am not good. I do not always do right. So, as a sinner, I pray you find me worthy through the extended grace and mercy you provide me daily. Lord, my husband left me, and although I have prayed for years that he become the man you called him to be, it wasn't until after our divorce that it came to fruition. The divorce made me realize I also have a calling on my life. You have called me for such a time as this to pen my story."*

The writing, journaling, praying, and fasting were all steps taken many years ago when I first thought of sharing my story of being a young, married mother. I wanted to share the challenges of day-to-day motherhood and, of course, being a wife. However, over the years, my story evolved into something much different.

The day came when my husband asked me for a divorce after 23 years of marriage. *The Other Side of Through* seemed like a fitting title for the story I did not know I would write. I found it interesting that God gave me the title **YEARS** before the fullness of my story actually manifested. I was afraid of the unknown. Fear rode shotgun as I tried to find my footing once again. How was I going to make it on my own?

"Lord, I have never been on a journey of this magnitude. I ask that you keep my thoughts as I write this book and allow the Holy Spirit to flow through my fingers so that the readers will get a revelation and a message from you. I desire to share my testimony that all things really do work together for our good!"

As I write this book, my thoughts travel back in time when I still find there are moments I must fight through the pain, confusion, and depression attached to the memories.

Rosemary Hill

*"As I type the last letter in my story, Lord, may it be all that you would have wanted me to share. I pray my journey will be a beacon of light to help others see their way to **The Other Side of Through**."*
Amen.

The Other Side Of Through

INTRODUCTION

After serving 15 years in the U.S. military and traveling to many places, I have encountered a variety of different cultures and environments. Ironically, it was through my family that I was exposed to the vast differences in people. While others blame discrimination and suppression of a particular sect of people, do not be fooled. Some of those closest to you have more of an influence over your perceptions than you may even realize.

The inspiration for this book came from the many women I have met along life's journey who look like me...on the **INSIDE**. While there are, of course, obvious differences on the outside, getting to know women from different cultures has been an amazing experience. I have learned that once we began to discuss current political or social events, our commonalities were revealed. It was through those discussions I learned how alike we were in ways I had never imagined.

When it came to the struggles with depression and hopelessness that stemmed from toxic relationships, it was as if I was peering into a mirror. Race, color, and economic status' light dimmed as each of us recognized the impartiality of our humanness as it related to being a woman in today's world.

Through this book, it is my hope and prayer that I can meet others in that 'dark place' and offer a word of encouragement that will get them through to the other side of what may be a place of misery; a place that sometimes feels like a plane in a holding pattern as they make a critical decision to continue on with this thing called 'LIFE'.

One of the most depressing times in my life as a Christian was not being able to exercise my faith. Faith has always been my weapon. I did not have to see it to believe it. Then, one day, my faith, hope, and joy tapped out. I found myself in the dark on my bathroom floor, praying for God to come down and manifest Himself to me. The dark is where so many of us experience loss, hurt, and shame. In that moment, I needed to know — without a shadow of a doubt — that all I had ever believed in by way of His Word was true. As I laid on that floor crying, although I did not see God, I felt the presence of another. Actually, it was not just one person; it was three to four women. *(I believe they were women, as I felt I was sharing that space with others whose faces I could not see, but whose spirits could relate to my own.)* I was comforted. I was not alone. My situation was not limited to me. Revelation came: There were others whom had not shared their story with me, and our meeting place would be in a dark space (not literally, but figuratively) with me leading the charge.

The Word of God says in Psalm 30:5, *"Weeping may endure for a night, but joy cometh in the morning."* Although darkness represents night, sometimes the pain and hurt when you are going through have a way of overextending themselves into the day. The good news is that morning is a representation of light, and where light is, darkness cannot share the same space. The two cannot exist together. As such, overcoming your hurt and pain is inevitable; it has to happen! God's Word does not lie! The situation may not improve immediately (and often not in a timing that is to our liking). In fact, it may get worse. Guess what? How you go through will change you and the way you confront every other trial you will face in life.

As I began to view my situations differently, I encouraged myself, which prompted the pressures 'of the dark' to lighten. I understood how pain looked, and when I saw it coming, I prepared myself for it. However, there were others times in my life when I was prayed up and steadfast, yet life had a way of presenting obstacles and challenges in spite of. I found myself feeling like the wind was knocked out of me. I am grateful for the fresh winds of grace and mercy that picked up speed and steadily strengthened! They held me up when I felt faint.

Allow those same winds to go beneath your wings. Allow them to lift your wings and head so that you can soar! Don't look for grace and mercy in a particular way because they will likely come in forms you were not even expecting.

To God be the **GLORY** for His grace, loving-kindness, and mercy! **Amen.**

"I pray that out of His glorious riches, He may strengthen you with power through His Spirit in your inner being…"
(Ephesians 3:16, NIV)

The Other Side Of Through

TABLE OF CONTENTS

DEDICATION .... **VI**

PREFACE .... **XXIV**

INTRODUCTION .... **XXVII**

THE BEST ME **1**

THE BROKEN ME **9**

MATTERS OF THE HEART **17**

SOMEONE HAS LEFT THE ROOM **25**

BE STILL **35**

BEND BUT DON'T BREAK **39**

LETTING GO, LETTING GOD **45**

LESSONS LEARNED **53**

UNTIL I GET IT OUT OF MY SYSTEM **61**

OPTIONS, OPTIONS, OPTIONS! **67**

FALLING BELOW GOD'S WILL **71**

CRAWL, WALK, RUN **81**

THE OTHER SIDE OF THROUGH **85**

CONCLUSION **99**

ABOUT THE AUTHOR **101**

Rosemary Hill

THE BEST ME

The days seem to go by quickly when there is so much going on in your life. The old saying, *"Time waits for no one"*, seems so relevant. After 22 years of marriage and three children, I sacrificed a lot of things in life to be a great role model and to be selfless in giving my children the best **ME** I could give.

My young adulthood was short-lived, but that was choice I made when I got pregnant at the age of nineteen. Although I was in the military and married to my child's father, it made for a good news story that we were making it happen. I struggled with learning about who this new me was. Living hundreds of miles — sometimes thousands of miles — away from home and being a young mother brought a lot of pressure to my life.

When I think about how I go through processes and react to situations, I think about how my mind takes me back to when I was a teenager, watching the adults around me go through their situations and deal with their life's challenges when it came to relationships. I quickly realized that it was a short thought, as it all seemed to be very confusing. Everything was hidden; *a secret.*

Now, I did understand that personal challenges are not to be put on display and are not everyone's business; however, toxic relationships are either emotionally or physically abusive. It seems that if there were issues with talk of infidelity or abuse, the discussion or advice was given by someone who did not have the right or skill to address it in a healthy way. With that, I never heard of anyone in my family going to see a therapist or marriage counselor. I believe my family responded to life's challenges and issues with the best intentions but not necessarily the best judgment. The problem is they were all matters of the heart. Too often, the hurt would get buried and resurface in the form of anger against others—not the person who caused the pain. I believe they were busy trying to be their best and do their best with each of their situations, which sometimes was very entertaining (depending on how deep the wound and who the individual was). It would signal different things to me about me and how they should act or care for their woman. Sometimes, it was like watching a reality show: entertaining but at some point, it quickly turned into *"God, help us all!"* moments.

Needless to say, watching the women in my family maneuver through their relationships and life's challenges was confusing. I would soon find out that relationships were not easy and that the women in my family were their best. They did teach me wonderful things about being a good person and how to take care of my family and myself, but I knew nothing and was not prepared to take care of my heart.

Leaving home to go into the military at the age of 19, I considered myself to be smart, disciplined, and determined…but I was not whole. I imagine that is to be expected; however, there was something about me that was broken. I know the word 'broken' is rather harsh and signifies some deeper issues and problems but continue reading, and you will find I had internal issues that would cause me not to be true to myself.

It was nothing my family did or did not do for me or to me. Rather, it was a conversation—a dialogue—about relationships and men that either I missed or subconsciously continued in a pattern of behavior.

The Other Side Of Through

When others my age ran off and refused to grow up quicker than they needed to, I was the one who said, *"No! I am going to commit to this life and this journey. I am going to do this the right way because I have been given this gift, this precious life, and I have to show God that I am grateful."* Well, as I went through this part of my challenging journey, I did not realize that my attempt to be the best mother I could be did not mean I had to lose sight of who I was. I always figured that if I be the best **ME**, I would be the best sister, the best wife, the best daughter, the best mother, and the best of the best! Trying to be all things to all people can be taxing and draining, to say the least.

Well, that didn't work because I began to overanalyze each and every situation and facet of my life. I am sure I drove my husband and others crazy with my paranoid behavior of doing "the right thing". *But why did I drive them crazy?* In my mind, I was striving to be the best me and maintain a balance of mind, body, and soul. My continued search to be the best me landed me in sultry company; the ones living adulteress lifestyles, getting drunk, and not serving God. Great. I found out I needed to change who I allowed to be in my life.

I thought I had found the best me in a church called "Genesis Church of God in Christ" that was located in Sierra Vista, Arizona. It was there, in a church with about 20 people, that I experienced God like I would never experience Him again: through the Holy Ghost and speaking in tongues. This would be a life-changing spiritual experience because to me, it gave me confirmation that I received evidence I was a child of the Most High and **HE** thought enough of me to show me His power. He allowed me to speak with Him in a language that, at this point, even I could not interpret.

The Other Side Of Through

The more I understood the things of God and established a personal relationship with Him, there grew a disconnect from my husband. Remember: I was trying to be the best me, dedicated mom, wife, and soldier. Why was this thing called "life" not working out for me? The question I still have today is: *Why did my quest to become whole and the "best me" cause me to become so paralyzed to the point I did not want to defend the **ME** I wanted to be?* The best me was suppressed by the women whom my husband cheated on me with. With each affair, I compromised who I wanted to become because each time, it took away my self-esteem and confidence. I told myself that each time I forgave him, I was not as important as the marriage and no matter what, the **BEST ME** would take the high road. I associated being the best me with being patient through unfair treatment by my husband.

That experience I had at church and the conversation I had with God would help me get through each storm.

You must understand that there will be a fight to do your best and be your best. There are a million distractions around us that cause us to lose focus and sight of what God has for us, but I encourage you to keep moving. When life knocks you down, keep getting up.

As I continued traveling to the other side of through, I have learned that the best me is not a "perfect me". This mindset has allowed me to be whole, have fun, and love who I am right now.

THE BROKEN ME

Just how many changes can we go through at one time?

When you give all of yourself to something or someone, it is at that point you become broken. There is nothing left for you to give back to yourself. Thank God, I worked an hour-and-a-half away from home, as I was able to muster up enough energy to put on my happy face and (sadly) enough praise to give God glory for keeping what was left of my mind.

Being broken due to my relationships — and life's challenges in general — made me wonder how I was able to give 100% of me in so many different areas. When I fell apart, I felt like nothing was going to go right. Where I was once able to balance going to school as a wife, mother, and full-time employee — and oh yeah: serve in church ministry without batting an eye or missing a beat...

STOP THE PRESS!

This husband of mine just may be cheating, **OR** my house has flooded, **OR** maybe all of those things at the same time. Let's add in the fact that the job I once loved has now become the most boring place on the planet.

Well, on the other side of all that was weighing me down, there was God—waiting to replenish me and restore things *NOT* back to the way they were, but to put the broken pieces back together to make a new model. The old model withstood the past hurts and experiences, but all that I had been asking for—a better job, a husband that would be a gentleman, and a new home were coming to pass. The scary part of that is I was not willing to let go of the old that made me so miserable because God: I just didn't add up!

I prayed and cried. I prayed and fasted. Then, I cried lots more, all the while petitioning the Lord to fix this stuff in my life. I think of Abraham when I think of my marriage because Abraham was asked to sacrifice his son and he said, *"Yes, Lord."* He did not think of **ALL** that he had done with and for his son. He did not think about **ALL** the praying he and his wife, Sarah, did to get that child. Abraham knew his child was a blessing from God, but God was trying to show him more.

I am going to flat out confess: I was scared to let go! I know that God didn't tell me to sacrifice my husband to show my faithfulness, but He did ask me if I loved my husband more than I loved Him! It is hard to trust the unknown because if it doesn't turn out how we would have wanted, we then beat ourselves up, pull out a bag, pack it up, and carry it around with us on to the next situation or relationship.

I learned that some things, God did not fix, allow, or trust me with until I showed I really believed Him for it all and that He truly was the Head of my life. Many times, I said, *"Lord, you are the Lord of lords and the King of kings. I trust you."* This was normally something I would say as part of a well-said prayer, as it sounded like something I saw in His Word, something I have heard being preached and prayed, or something that sounded good rolling off my tongue.

The sad news is that we say a lot of things such as what we won't tolerate, but the truth of the matter is we cannot say we stand on God's Word when we are going through — unless we are tried by the Spirit. If I am still, God will put me back together the way I was intended to be put together so that I can move on to what He has in store for me. This broken state is so sensitive because there are times the flesh wants to do things that are not very Christ-like.

Admittedly, I fell apart when I lost track of who I was as an individual. It's funny: I was supporting everyone else by encouraging them to be the best person they could be yet I forgot to keep myself relevant. I became a wife, mother, co-worker, daughter, sister...you name it; I had a title for it. The most important title was lost: **ME**.

When my oldest went off to school, my title of 'mother' seemed to shrink a little. Don't get me wrong: She still needed me, and I was still there, but she was not in the home anymore. Then, she started calling less and less. Then, my son left home after graduation. My role as 'mom' became smaller. ***THEN***, all at once, my husband left, and the title of 'wife' left me altogether. I had a reminder by the name of Amber Hill who, at the tender age of 16, became my rock. There were days when she would come home from school and find me still in bed with not much life left in me. My heart was so heavy that when I did get out of bed, it was as though I had a rock chained to me that made the simplest of tasks exhausting.

I remember during the winter months when the snow would fall, instead of getting dressed like I normally would, I would choose to dress in my flannel pajamas, comb my hair, and put on my pearls. This was my winter outfit for the day, especially when we were snowed in. My daughter knew that this was something I enjoyed and although not wintry outside, there was a heavy snowstorm taking place in my heart.

One afternoon, she asked me, *"Mom, are you going to get up and put on your pajamas and pearls today?"* I replied, *"Yes, baby girl. That is a good idea."* Recalling this time in my life reminds me of the biblical story of Joseph. He was thrown into a pit after being sold as a slave by his brothers. The threat of who Joseph was was so great, it caused his own flesh and blood to turn against him.

My husband leaving after over 20 years of marriage caused me to spiral down into a pit of depression. In my mind, he left me for dead in the pit because he did not care about the impact his leaving had on me. He knew how much I loved him. Now that I am on the other side, I can appreciate his strength and the courage it took to leave me in search for what made him whole and happy. There is a way to settle disputes and unhappiness in a relationship, so I do not condone his actions and how he exited the marriage. I learned that I am responsible for my happiness, but God gave me joy. Happiness is temporary, and that is what I had with him in our marriage. I did not experience joy with him. In fact, I have yet to experience unconditional love in a relationship.

I know that someone reading this can relate to this dark in which we may have met. If so, I pray that you, too, are reading this because you made it to the other side of through. If you are reading this and are currently in this dark place, I encourage you to get up, get dressed, put on the attire of your choice, and keep your feet moving. The other side of through is only a few "feet" away! It is time that you be made whole.

MATTERS OF THE HEART

One day while at work, my brother was hospitalized with a life-threatening illness. His health really started to diminish. My mother and I were told by the doctors (via a phone call) that he may only have a few days left and that if we wanted to see him, we needed to get there as soon as possible. After our call with the doctor, I spoke with my mother about the logistics of flying out to where my brother was. I sat in my office for a moment just staring out the window, stunned at the news I just received. It began to sink in that I was about to lose my brother. I had lost my older brother a few years prior, and my mind quickly turned to what my mother must have been going through at that moment.

Speaking of death, I was dealing with something dead of my own: my marriage.

After a few moments, I called my husband and explained to him what was going on with my brother. By this time, it was about 1:00 in the afternoon and I imagined that he would come home *immediately* after work to console me and continue helping me figure things out, but I was disappointed **again**. He did not show up until after 9:00 p.m. that night. He stated that the guys at work wanted to take him out for his birthday that was coming up in a few days. I could not understand how celebrating his birthday trumped being by my side when I needed him.

Nevertheless, my mom and I flew to where my brother was and began making the necessary arrangements to bury him, given the doctor's diagnosis. My first day there, after conducting business all that morning with my mom, we went to the hospital to spend time with my brother. It was there I received a phone call from my husband stating he wanted to talk to me.

The Other Side Of Through

Although I had *just* left home the day before, I jumped at the chance to do so because he did not like to talk. In fact, I had been trying to get him to let me know what was going on with him.

I left the hospital room and went to sit in the rental car in the parking garage to see what he wanted to talk about. I called him back, and when he didn't initially ask how my family or I was doing, I discerned that the conversation was not going to be good. I never imagined that it would take the turn that it did.

He began to tell me how unhappy he was, but that I was a good woman. Then, he said, *"I just can't do this anymore."* He told me that when I returned home, he was leaving.

Dealing with matters of the heart and family can be difficult. When you lose someone, it can put stress on every fabric of your life. Your entire life changes and, at that moment, I was losing a brother **AND** a husband. I did what I knew all too well to do: cry and pray. But then, I laughed! For the first time, I really felt that my life was meaningful because I said, *"It's time to go to war! If I am going to survive this, I will need to be focused. And although I will feel faint and weak from this broken heart I was experiencing, I am not giving up right now."* I believed (again) that God would not allow this. If there would be a victory, it would require a lot of fasting and praying.

I exited the car doing something I would have to perfect so that the world would not know how shattered I was inside: I squared my shoulders, made sure the clasp on my pearls was in the center of the back of my neck, took a deep breath, and went back into the hospital. I did not share with anyone the conversation I had and continued to help my mother and visit my family. Later, I called my therapist who I had been seeing and asked if she had an appointment available on the day I was to return. I briefly told her what took place. She prayed with me and told me to hang in there. My brother began to show signs of getting better, and after a few days, the doctors regained hope that he would pull through. With my brother not really out of the woods, my mom and I left, but everything was in order.

When I returned home, my husband picked my mom and me up from the airport as if nothing was wrong. I remember him **not** greeting me with a hug or warm *"Welcome back!"* He kind of ignored me and spoke directly to my mom, asking how the flight was. After we dropped her off at home, we continued on to our home — almost in silence, until I asked where our youngest daughter was and why she did not come with him. He explained that she was at a football game with her classmates and nothing more. I was in shock that he did not show any compassion or empathy for me. It was like I had done something terrible to him and he was just disgusted with me. Once we arrived home, I asked if we could discuss why he felt it was appropriate to tell me he was leaving while I was away dealing with the potential loss of my brother. He said he just could not *"do this"* anymore and that he was not happy. I imagine the unhappiness did not happen overnight, considering he had already moved into our guest bedroom.

I ignored the warning signs, bad dreams, discernment, and gut feelings because I was so willing to pray for him when he was having bad days and going through a period in his life where he was confused. However, if someone loves and cares for you, they will put their feelings in check and do whatever it takes to keep you in their life. They will not let you go, push you away, or deny how they feel, especially when it hurts the other person. There is something I have learned about love and that is there is always one who loves more than the other. The worse feeling is investing days, months, and years by depositing emotions into a bank—only to find out there are insufficient funds when you go to make a withdrawal.

Dealing with the loss of a loved-one is extremely difficult; however, I have found it worse to deal with the loss of someone you love that is still very much alive. When someone walks away from you or out of your life, it is heartbreaking. Although the emotions can be described, the pain in your heart is indescribable.

Matters of the heart are complicated, so when emotions and your heart are involved, just remember that the heart that matters is your own! Although I felt that this was about me being "not enough", nothing was wrong with me. I was beautiful; always have been. I was smart; always have been.

SOMEONE HAS LEFT THE ROOM

About a year prior to my husband leaving me, the intimacy and communication stopped, but rejection and depression came to take their place. I blamed myself and felt that he was bored with me, so I found myself at times going into my closet to cry and pray. The closet was that dark space I could find even in the middle of a bright, sunny day. I would sit under the clothes that hung from the rack and almost found it ironic that the clothes I used to cover my body to protect me from the outside elements and my nakedness were being used to hide **ME**. I liked this place because it made me feel as though I was shutting out the world. I wanted nothing more than to be alone. It also provided a space for me to cry without my daughter hearing me. However, one day when I went into the closet, I had cried and prayed for so long, I fell asleep—only to be awakened by her calling my name. I quickly came out so that she wouldn't know I was in there, much like the closet in my mind when I would leave home to go work, church, or wherever I did not want others to know my inner struggle and the magnitude of it.

There were times when I would be so very present physically and even laughing with others while my mind was filled with thoughts of being ignored by my husband, feeling inadequate and worthless. I thought of ways to change his heart. My default was always to pray. I could not figure this out and began to believe that this was a spiritual battle that I could not fight in the natural. Looking back, I always had a mustard seed of faith, and with that little bit of faith, I called out to God and reminded Him of His Word. I would quote scriptures and cast the works of the enemy down; however, that was not enough to keep him. Eventually, he left. I questioned if God heard me at all.

I know many of us believers have been tried and tested in situations. You may be facing one even now. I challenge you to take a look around and remind yourself each moment that you are more than a conqueror and that this, too, shall pass. Easier said than done; I know. But let me share with you an encounter I had with a few women I do not know.

After my husband left, I was so depressed, I could not eat or sleep. I would try my best to pick myself up by taking a nice, hot shower. Initially, it was soothing and would calm me down, but one day, I found myself crying even in the shower. At least there, my tears would blend in with the water from the shower.

I would continuously ask God, *"How? Why me?"* I could not grasp that his leaving was not about me but about his desire to be alone and see what life was like without me. A part of me even thought I was being selfish for begging him to stay when so many times before, not only did he show me he did not want the marriage; I also had enough discernment to know that the past was just too much to get over these things — combined with the dreams (or nightmares) of seeing him with another woman.

One particular time, I took a shower to calm myself down. I found myself crying yet again. I had gotten so upset and worked up, I immediately got out of the shower and could barely dry off because I felt very weak. I began to hyperventilate. Almost dizzy, I put on my robe and sat on the floor next to the tub in the master bedroom. Tears flowed and flowed down my face as though I was still in the shower. I again called and cried out to God and, as I laid my head against the tub with eyes still closed, I took a deep breath and sat in silence. There was a calmness, a peaceful energy that fell upon me. I then began to feel that there were other people in the room with me.

First, it was the presence of other people in the room; then it was the distinct feeling of other women. I was confused by the whole thing, but then it came to me that I was not the only person experiencing this sadness; other women were suffering just like I was. I was not the only woman feeling rejected and experiencing sadness or depression. Neither was I the only woman whose husband had left them after 20 years of marriage. These women seemed real to me. Their presence and energy felt real.

But then, something happened. I felt as though someone had left the room. This person who left seemed to have an amazingly strong presence that was so noticeable, I opened my eyes and looked around the bathroom as if awakened from a deep sleep. Although my eyes were opened, I continued in my thoughts about what just happened: the feeling of the other ladies in the other ladies in the room but more importantly, the one who left. I thought maybe she found a way out from underneath all this rubble of hurt or maybe someone came to her out of her dark place.

Looking back, I think that woman was me; not having found a way out nor did someone come for me. Rather, it was with the understanding that I was not alone in this and others were suffering. I decided to continue my journey.

Many of you reading this were there for this part of my journey. However, there are some things I am sharing for the first time that you may not know. I would be remiss if I did not say that this story, along with others in this book, is being shared so that it may help someone. It's not meant to hurt, degrade, or paint a bad picture of anyone.

Fast-forward about six months. I had just arrived at my new place of employment and I, of course, did not know anyone. In the coming hours or days, people would soon find out who I was. You see, I had unknowingly accepted a job at the very place my ex-husband had recently resigned from. His resignation was due to a compromising situation in which he thought it was in his best interest to leave on his own accord. Well, that 'compromising situation' was a co-worker he was intimately involved with. The co-worker, however, continued to work at this location and, after I arrived, I had to see her just about every day (mostly in passing). It was tough for me to get up every morning and go to work, knowing I would see this young lady.

If you don't know by now, I *love* pearls. They give me a feeling of power and control over my emotions and thoughts. As I got into my car each morning, I would pray the entire way there, asking God to hold back the tears and even take away the pain. There was about a week straight that whenever I arrived and got out of my vehicle, I would see her in the parking lot. What a way to start the morning! I was on my new job, wanting to prove myself and make a good impression, yet I am about to lose my mind from seeing this person whom my husband was living with. **YES.** *Did you catch that?* Each morning I saw her, it ripped my heart out to know she had just left him…just talked to him. I have no doubt he told her to have a good day. And me? I was alone.

I would greet people, and they would ask in return, *"How are you?"* No one had a clue that I was on the verge of a nervous breakdown. I would share my past work history and experiences and offer up creative solutions to my customers, all the while clutching my pearls as I made my way to my car to break down and cry from the pain. When I could not make it to my car, I would go to the restroom or simply close my office door to release whatever pain I could, so that I could take the next step or next breath.

No one knew how much I was suffering. After all, I did not know them, and they did not know me. Still, they all asked me how I was doing, and we exchanged smiles.

To those who may feel as though you are the only one going through this, first off: **You are wrong.** There were so many negative feelings wrapped up in this short chapter, but the feeling of *depression* is real. I think we all struggle with it in some form but some struggle harder than others. For me, it was clearly situational and driven by this horrific separation and divorce after 23 years, and although there are times it rears its ugly head, I have found ways to deal with it.

The most important was is **NOT ALONE.**

BE STILL

I'm nervous. I'm scared. I want it to be over. The following analogy comes to mind: I feel as though I'm standing in the eye of the storm, that peaceful place that has utter destruction going on all around me.

With all that my husband I have been through, who would have thought we would be here…in *THIS* place. *THIS* place represents hurt, anger, manipulation, disconnection, shattered promises, and broken marriage vows. It also represents sin, shame, and guilt.

In the midst of it all, God is here. He has been here all the time! His Word tells us that He is the Author and Finisher of our faith. He is the Beginning and the End. That means He is in the midst of **ALL** my circumstances!

Sidebar: On this day of writing, my husband gave me my ring back, and I was asked to be his wife again. It was not what I imagined, and for a second, I thought it was more for "show". In all honesty, I'm not sure this is what I want, but for now, I relish in the moment of peace—even if it is not the peace that passes all understanding.

Moving forward...

Sometimes, I get so focused on what I want, need, and feel I deserve that I miss God's voice. I'm sure He is whispering to me, *"MY TIME and MY WILL, MY CHILD. Let Me complete this work in your husband that I began. Just **BE STILL**."*

The mind is amazing. Like the tongue, it can be creative and bring forth life **AND** death. The death I am referring to is the death **IN** (not *OF*) our lives and the lives of others. I was living with this man for years, and in his mind, he did not want me to be here. He was thinking about death of the marriage, leaving all that we built behind.

I entered into this storm expecting the victory, so I speak to this storm and tell it to get out of my way so that I will have love, peace, and true joy. Above all else, may God's glorious works break and shine through the stormy skies!

Rosemary Hill

"Be still, and know that I am God…"
(Psalm 46:10, NIV)

BEND BUT DON'T BREAK

I know that in life, we must remain flexible to change. Whether it is change on the job, school, home, or getting older, let's face it: If ever anything in life was constant, it would be *change*.

It is amazing the things we will do to have something that is not even authentic. We will stretch, bend, and even break our backs to keep someone in our lives, all for what seems to be the appearance of having a relationship. For me, it was better than not having one at all.

Being in a relationship for 23 years — good, bad, or indifferent — and having someone there is a lot to let go of because although I would find out about different women my husband had been with, the unhealthy and dysfunctional cycle was like being on a rollercoaster that I could not get off and was *scared* to get off. I learned how to deal with the occurrences, as crying and praying became all too natural. The pain, depression, and neglect that came with it, however, would cause me to reach that breaking point and would ultimately stay with me long after he left. There are a few dependent variables or elements I became dependent on, and when it was no longer there, it was a strain. An example was becoming a single parent and being responsible for the entire household budget when we built our kingdom with two incomes. Early in the marriage, it frightened me to imagine ending my marriage while I had three children at home. Although life would not have been lonely, financially alone, it would have been harder.

I spent a lot of time on bended knees reminding myself that the Word of God says in Hebrews 13:5, *"God will never leave me nor forsake me."* Yet there were so many days and nights when I felt so alone and, at times, abandoned. It was because I took God's Word and expected my husband to be what God says He would be to me. I know now that I took my eyes off God and was focused entirely too much on keeping a man who God may have been trying to save me from so that I would live out my destiny. My praise and exultation were to God for what He had given me, yet I felt like I could not live without this man. *Could it be that I was only giving God praise and worshipping Him because I needed him to fix the marriage or was it simply because He was God all by Himself?*

I do not want to discount the relationship I had with my husband because my feelings were real. They were feelings I had for a man whom God joined together with me to be what was supposed to be a lifetime. I cuddled up with a mindset that good, bad, or indifferent, I was with this man "until death do us part". I soon found myself exhausted from lack of emotions and loneliness from not interacting with the world. My world was here with my family.

I had been in worship and asking God to please let me know what it is like to feel the love of a man as a woman. I needed to know what it felt like to have a man in love with **ME**. Is that possible? Well, the response I received was remarkable!

God revealed to me that I will not know the love of a man until I began to appreciate the love **HE** has given (and continues to give) me already. I do not have anything concrete to base the love on; nothing to compare it to. After all, I never really had it. I thought that any love was better than what my husband had given me…but not necessarily.

As I worked through my hurt, I began speaking to and chatting with my ex-husband. We were able to form a friendship. The cordial and casual conversations came only after I was able to *forgive* him. This was necessary in order to co-parent my youngest daughter. The fact that he was living with another woman was enough for me to broaden my heart's decision to leave him behind. No longer do I desire to be with him, which is in stark contrast to the days when I considered him my best friend.

I have turned down many advances during the hurtful times in my marriage. There are some I am sure would have taken care of and loved me, but my loyalty to my marriage vows and belief in God would not let me leave. Even after the emotional and physical abuse, I did not know *how* to leave. I always say that he did something I could never do: **LEAVE.**

Thinking back, I believe God *allowed* our separation and divorce. He heard my heart's cry not to feel abandoned and unloved by a man who was responsible for taking care of me and loving me as he loved himself. I did not want to be the 'other woman'. There were too many women who have shared my life and my marriage. Too many have left their perfume smells on my husband's laundry. Even today, their scents linger with the memories I cannot shake; however, the perfume smells, and the bad memories are fading away with each step I take towards wholeness. With each fresh dose of grace and mercy given to me daily by God, my hope is being restored. The other side of through is near!

Don't just be open to change; be flexible, being careful to bend…**but don't break!**

LETTING GO, LETTING GOD

At the time, my husband seemed confused. For a while, I watched as he tossed and turned with the idea and thoughts of leaving. At the same time, God revealed to me in dreams that he would leave, but I chose to hang on for dear life. I held on to the idea that the marriage would miraculously be saved, like it was my lifeboat in the middle of an ocean. The problem with that was my husband had already drifted away.

I was in the boat by myself.

There is a saying that if you let something go and it returns, then it was meant for you. I must say that even if my ex-husband returns, I don't see me accepting him back. I think God allowed all of this to happen so that I could be released from all that concerned me, just so He could continue to perfect the work in me that He started.

The Word of God says to *"speak those things that are not as though they were"*, but I made a cardinal mistake: I covered up all the dysfunctionality in my marriage with scripture. There is a difference; therefore, knowing when to let go is **extremely** important. I thought that because I was a wife and that if I did thing pretty close to perfect, I would be blessed. I think of all the good I did to make the marriage work and to make our house a home. It saddens me, as I feel I did it in vain and that it was unappreciated. To say or think I did those things to be appreciated or loved more or as a way of showing my commitment is a bit twisted.

Having strong women in my life now has helped me refocus on what is important so that I am not out wandering aimlessly after this storm.

Those I mentioned in the Dedication of this book all came to my rescue when they saw me injured and in need of prayer, support, and friendship. Their insights and perspectives were helpful because they saw things I could not, such as seeing that I was a strong woman and not only did I deserve better, but God had something greater in store for me.

I chose not to take the long road to recovery and getting back to life after being hospitalized. It was essential that I "hurried". I had a new job and a daughter that still needed her mother. Although I fainted in this process, I was not the only one affected by it. In all that I had to get back to, I still needed to go through the healing process. The "letting go and letting God" process is what I call it. I believe that each process in and of itself can truly be a journey. Getting "through" is the goal.

Because I am a visual person, I like to "see" things. There is also a part of me that likes to "control" things. I like to see things so that I can have hope that it is so; the Word of God, however, says **nothing** at all about *seeing* but states emphatically that *"faith cometh by hearing and hearing by the Word of God."* The controlling part of me (at this point) wants to make sure I don't get hurt again. I do not allow someone to come into my life—man or woman—and wound me the way I was wounded. I do not doubt that if I don't let go and let God, this could very well happen again. Because I lost sight of God and did not seek Him first, things were not added unto me; they were taken away.

Although I am sure I have a sad story to share here in this chapter, I think sharing my perspective on "letting go and letting God" is a little more important because it involved destiny.

The Other Side Of Through

There are **hundreds** of books on the market written by famous writers that will give the same message (maybe with a little more flare); however, my words are from my trials and tribulations and my heart of hearts. You see, I have read some of those books and found they were way above my level of understanding. I needed a book that, when I read it, I could see the author was writing from a place in which I had been or perhaps was at the time. I needed to read about a woman in the storm, trapped in a cycle of depression, low self-esteem, a place of hopelessness, emotionally distraught, and abused; a place where this precious thing called "life" just did not make sense nor was it a place they wanted to be. Then, as the book progressed, I needed to see that they rose above the depression and survived the process of healing and overcoming.

That was the story I needed to read. **This** is the story I present to you.

Maybe the things written here are simple to some, and because you know me, you bought the book. However, there is someone who will pick up this book and, in one or several chapters, find that they can survive their storm and learn that the victory is in each second, minute, hour, and day that we decide to let go of the past. She will get better and not become bitter because of the scars and wounds received in the battle. Many of those scars are not seen with the visual eye, but they most certainly are there.

If you are seeing to "let go" of someone, first determine what it is that you are letting go. For me, it was initially the tangible things. I needed to remove everything in the home that belonged to him. Well, being that we were married for so long, I found that my home would be empty if I continued doing that. As I went through the hurt and healing process, I found that as I shed the emotional and intangibles, those were the things that indicated I was letting go. No matter what I saw in the home — a picture, a tool, a chair — they didn't bother me because I let go of the emotions tied to those things.

I remember talking to God and asking Him to remove certain things and feelings from my life that were not like Him. With prayer being nothing more than a discussion with God, I asked Him to do it at the same time, understanding that it would mean a void would become present with that removal. The hurt and pain of letting go of someone or something can be difficult, even traumatic; but as I prayed, God responded by filling that void with blessings and love.

No matter what 'ship' — friendship or relationship — you may find yourself in, do not settle because in settling, you "sit". Keep your feet moving. Remember: In order to get to the other side, the journey requires that you keep moving. Trust me: I know the comfort in "at least having someone" in your life; however, if you are going to hurt, decide to hurt one good and last time. Hurt as you heal. Letting go requires that you give up something. In my case, it was giving it "up" to God, the One who has all power and from whom **ALL** blessings flow.

LESSONS LEARNED

Praying to God and asking Him to touch the heart of my husband so that he would see me and love me became a routine prayer. While married, I tried several times to get my husband to go to therapy with me and probably like most men, he declined every time. I asked him to talk to someone at our church (like one of the ministers or the pastor), and it was something he would not do, even if it meant saving the marriage. I respected his decision but did not stop pressing the issue, so I asked if he had a close friend he trusted to be a neutral party or just listen to him about what he was struggling with.

Sometimes, I would look at my husband, and it was like watching a bad movie when you can see the person with the knife about to attack someone from behind. You yell at the screen, *"TURN AROUND!"* Likewise, I could see the spiritual attack of the enemy and would tell him *(I am sure to him, it was just me nagging or trying to use something spiritual to control him).*

After my failed attempts to get him to talk to someone, I let it go. You know: One of those "let go and let God" moments. I seemed to want a breakthrough more for him than he wanted it for himself. To be honest, I spent more time praying he would give his life to Christ and that he would be delivered from the strongholds that had him bound and were destroying our marriage. All the while, I should have been praying that I would be delivered, healed, and set free from some things myself.

Lesson learned: Put on my own mask before I try to put on someone else's.

Finally, I decided to go to therapy alone. Through a friend, I was given the name of a Christian Family Therapist by the name of Dr.

Judy Jacobs. Even though I was at the end of my rope and out of hope, Dr. Jacobs—who is a **phenomenal** woman of God—made it easy for me to let her into my world of depression, hurt, and hopelessness. The moment I met her, I knew this was where I was supposed to be; under her care and prayer. After I visited her a few times, I would tell him about the easy-going conversations. Eventually, he agreed to go with me to see her. His initial visit, he had with her alone. The following session, we met with her together.

We explored the foundation of our marriage and friendship. We learned and relearned things about one another. We talked about how our upbringings shaped us, how it influenced the way we formed opinions and made decisions, and how we placed things and life in order of importance. We learned about our love language and that it was not *ONE* specific thing that landed us in her office. Rather, it was the day-to-day demands of life and not making time for each other that certainly did not help.

I learned that I was tired of being the "spiritual head" of the house. It caused our home to be imbalanced. Even more conflict was created when I earned my degrees and received promotions. I served my husband and was very submissive to him, but there were times when I had to make decisions in his absence or times when the bond with the children showed itself strong with the guidance and closeness I shared with them. I could sense he felt as though they respected me in a different way, but again, this was established through the bond we formed on car rides, going to church, and praying together.

Being a woman of faith, I learned that no matter what my struggle was, I would never interfere with the bond my children shared with their father. The Word of God says in Exodus 20:10 to always promote honor and respect. Exodus 20:12 says to *"Honor your father and your mother, so that you may live long in the land the LORD your God is giving you."*

After only a few visits, my husband decided he no longer wanted to go to therapy. He was not ready to stop running from his truth and issues with infidelity. He expressed to me that he felt as though the therapist favored me and that somehow, he was not being treated fairly. I offered for us to go to another therapist, but he declined.

It wasn't that she favored me; she knew through spiritual discernment and being an expert in her field, what was going on with him. He was simply uncomfortable because many of the things she would say to him, he had already heard them from me. It gave me confirmation that when I spoke to him, it **WAS** from my heart of hearts as a person who cared very much about his *soul* — not just as a wife losing her husband. As much hurt, pain, and hell I was going through, I cared that my husband and friend was spiraling out of control. Nothing good was going to come from the path he was on.

I continued to go to therapy on my own, even after he left me. I remember at the beginning of one of my sessions, asking the therapist if she minded that we didn't talk about him anymore. In all I had learned on this journey, I wanted to know what it was about me that made me accept the things I accepted. What was it about me that did not teach him how to treat met? Why didn't I leave *years* ago?

There were so many lessons learned about what he did, but I was ready to be held accountable about what I did to **ME**. I was

determined to become better and not bitter. I did not have all the answers, but I learned enough to know I had a calling on my life.

"The Other Side of Through" was my destination.

Rosemary Hill

"The Lord makes firm the steps of the one who delights in Him; though he may stumble, he will not fall, for the Lord upholds him with His hand."
(Psalm 37:23-24, NIV)

UNTIL I GET IT OUT OF MY SYSTEM

I am not alone in that I have suffered with low self-esteem, rejection, and emotional abuse. I have met women who were extremely gorgeous and saw some of the same qualities, characteristics, and dysfunctions mentioned. Although our testimonies are different, the heartbreak is nevertheless the same because these things know no beauty, nationality, or social class.

My testimony to you is just that: **MY TESTIMONY**. The truth of the matter is we all have testimonies of overcoming trials and tribulations, but someone is reading this book who is gaining strength after coming out of a storm and who needs to know that letting go and healing is a process that differs from person to person. I emphatically believe that you must work through some feelings, behaviors, and habits. Get them out of your system! You are not alone and should not trade in hurt and pain for guilt and shame.

I made the mistake of giving someone "one more chance" to make sure I had exhausted all means and measures to make things work. I defined love in this manner, and the harsh reality was that the more I loved and sacrificed for the marriage and fought to keep my husband in my life, I was slowly losing who I was. I became less important, and without him, I was nothing. I even wanted to continue in the dysfunctional marriage. The quality of the relationship did not matter to me.

I was praying so hard for God to save my marriage when I was the one who needed to be saved.

I was focused on my husband loving me, instead of understanding the love of God.

The Other Side Of Through

I was sad over what I was losing and not appreciative of the things I was gaining, like peace, love, and joy.

I did not cry over the self-love I did not have.

I did not care that my relationship with my God was being neglected because I was at a place where I loved my husband more than God.

I was willing to kill myself; hence, I would have killed this message of hope and encouragement I share with you today.

Now, my change did not happen overnight. I am **still** learning how not to make some of the same mistakes of loving someone so hard and making those big deposits, only to get nothing in return.

It is natural to cling to an ideology you have held onto for years. The process of detaching yourself from love additions is important and a necessary part of the journey. Most people say, *"Just let it go!"* Let's face it: Those same people are attached to something, too—just not the same thing as you. I have heard comments such as, *"I cannot imagine what you are going through"*, *"You know; maybe it's best"*, and *"God has something greater for you."* All may be very true, but please: If this is your advice to me, give me a word of hope that keeps me afloat when I feel like I am drowning in pain and sorrow from this loss. As you ever-so-casually tell me to 'let it go', leave me with a joke that will make me smile or laugh to help me get through the thoughts of ending my life—the one where I'm being used, mistreated, and abandoned. Finally, do not walk away from me before showing me a few breathing techniques that will help me get through the next second or minute when I lose my breath at the mere *thought* of how I am going to make sure my daughter and I don't miss a meal or mortgage payment.

It seems quite simple to some people when it's clearly an unhealthy situation; but fear and doubt paralyze you, and even the Word of God that you may know so well makes it all seem insurmountable. You cannot always go "cold turkey" and turn off emotions and idea of someone or something. It is just not realistic!

So, keep going! Until you get it out of your system, keep checking your phone a million times per hour to see if that person has tried to reach out to you. Every time they don't, begin praying for God to help you **NOT** to seek something that, for one, is not there and, more importantly, that is not in His will for you.

This process takes time, so take that mustard seed of faith mentioned in Matthew

17:20 and plant it right there. Keep checking the emails and texts. Keep looking out the window until the desire to do so goes away. This is your hurt. The way you let it go is up to you. It is a process, and if you can rid yourself of it overnight, that may signal that there was no real attachment there at all.

The important part of this journey for me was learning that God loved me coming to Him each time I checked the message and nothing was there because I spoke to Him each time. This made my relationship with God stronger because as I was decreasing and detaching from one thing, I was increasing my time with God and connecting with Him without even realizing I was doing it! I was getting it out of my system!

OPTIONS, OPTIONS, OPTIONS!

After every affair, I had an option to stay or leave the marriage. *I stood firmly on the Word of God and believed He could fix my marriage.*

Once he moved into the guest room, I had the options of letting go, stop praying for a change, and giving up. *I stood firmly on the Word of God and believed He could fix my marriage.*

When he rejected me, I had the options of letting go, stop praying for a change, and giving up. *I stood on the Word of God and believed He could fix my marriage.*

When he scheduled dates with me and never showed up, I had the option of letting go, stop praying for a change, and giving up. *I believed God could fix my marriage.*

When he packed his things and took all he owned, *I fainted.*

The marriage was over. My heart was filled with hopelessness, shame, guilt, and resentment towards God. A million questions flooded my soul, all beginning with **"WHY?"** I almost died. My testimony almost died with me; it almost died **IN** me. *I had the option to trust God.*

We all have burdens to bear, but God instructs us in His Word to cast all of our burdens and cares upon Him (1 Peter 5:7). Our journeys are unique and, in the midst, we must recognize that we are not here to make anyone else better or save them. We are here to be a blessing to others; not to make them into something they are not.

Oh, what a **MESS** to pray something for someone that they have not asked you to pray for!

The Other Side Of Through

Praying that my husband became a better man for me was something that, although good, he did not want for himself. He had an option and did not choose me.

God has shown me that He loves me through my bountiful blessings. He has chosen me for such a time as this. There very fact that I am still here to write about my journey is a testament of how much He pursued me and didn't leave me. That kind of pursuit is unimaginable! God set the standard!

I must keep my focus on God and choose Him **every** time. I must understand that God's heavenly, divine love and courtship with Jesus, the Prince of Peace, are the marks for which I should reach. To think that any man can fill *GOD'S* shoes is **ludicrous**!

Along the way, I had to learn the role of being a helpmate **AND** to whom I am to be a helpmate for. Worshipping God in spirit and in truth (John 4:24) is being truthful about the open doors that we stand in front of, fearful to walk through.

I had the option to live or die (so I thought) until I was reminded that my life is not my own and that:

"The thief cometh not but to steal and to kill and to destroy. But Jesus came so that I might have life and have it more abundantly" (John 10:10).

Life is my **ONLY** option. Promise me you will make it your **ONLY** option as well.

FALLING BELOW GOD'S WILL

The Word of God says in Romans 3:23 that **ALL** have sinned and fallen short of the glory of God. I have lived my life thus far considering a lot of things and other people while putting myself last. In all I have done to please others and make them happy, I never knew how to make myself happy. I would like to believe that making others happy essentially brought me happiness. In theory, it sounds good. The reality is that it does not. Happiness is just an emotion one feels. It was really **JOY** I should have been praying for, which is an *experience*. I believe God finds favor in the way we care for our neighbors and extend a helping hand to others, but I am not convinced that God would have me neglect myself.

As I look back on the way I treated my husband, I should not be surprised that he put his needs above mine. I did, after all, do the same thing. His sometimes-narcissistic ways were a by-product of how I placed him on a pedestal. No matter what he did, I forgave him and hid the hurt in my heart because in my mind, at least I had someone…and no one is perfect.

Well after the many times I forgave the extra-marital affairs, I found myself at the end of my rope. This particular affair was not only the one that ended the marriage; it was also the one that would break me. I know in the previous chapter, I shared with you that these marital issues would test, stretch, and bend me in ways I could not imagine, but *THIS* is the one that made me lose my footing **and** my faith.

My husband worked and became romantically-involved with this young lady while we were still married (our divorce was pending). He moved in with her as though they were "just roommates", but the previous signs said otherwise.

He would like me to believe that she was not the reason he left. Maybe she wasn't, but the way it all happened gave it the appearance that this was the case. Even after moving in with another woman, I was willing to take this man back.

Many who know this story commended me for what I did next.

My husband and this young lady had an altercation at their home. He had to go to the police station because he was accused of domestic violence. When he called me and told me what happened, I asked him several times if he did any of the things she claimed. He told me no and that she was upset that he talked to her about leaving and coming back home to me.

WOW! I did *NOT* see that one coming—especially since the divorce had only been finalized a few weeks prior.

So, I went down to the police station with him, prayed with him, and sat with him until 4:00 a.m. the next morning when he was cleared to leave.

Needless to say, I got no sleep and, in a few hours, I would unknowingly have an interview at the same location where both of them worked! Due to the dynamics of where I work, it was not immediately known that this was the case.

Before leaving the police station, I invited him to come stay at home—in the basement—until things cooled off or he found a place to stay. I did not want to see him get into any more trouble with this woman. After all, he is the father of my children and, after 23 years, the loyalty and commitment were still there for me — even as the ink continued to dry on the divorce papers.

After convincing me that this thing was over between the two of them, things cooled off, and he took some time to get his head straight, we worked things out. I could painfully see that he either missed her dearly, did not want to be with me, or he just longed to be by himself. He looked very sad but stated it was because he was disappointed that he had allowed his life to spiral downward in this area. He admitted to having issues and that maybe he was narcissistic. Well, he had all the signs of one…I mean textbook!

A few months later, after many talks and spending a little more time with me, I started to fall below God's will. I ignored all the discernment and signs that this was only temporary and that things were not going to get better. He eventually moved out of my basement after about a week and returned to 'their' apartment. About a month later, he found a place of his own that he invited me to several times.

One day, I went there on a Friday when traffic was really heavy. Instead of a two-hour commute, I had an early dinner with him and went to his place to spend the remainder of time watching a movie. While there, I received a message from this young lady in response to a message I had sent her several months ago regarding her participation in the affair and telling her what she had done to my family. She went on to say how they were still together. I told her I was at his place that very moment and he was expressing wanting his family back. She asked me why I was at his home, and it made me feel so small. I was married to him when they started this mess, and she had the **NERVE** to question me? Her words began to make me feel as though I never mattered in the marriage and that for all these years, I was the 'other woman'.

Eventually, she showed up at his door. At first, he refused to let her in. I told him if he didn't, I was leaving. This was his opportunity to tell her about his desire to "fix things" with me and rebuild the family he tore apart.

The discussion was had. He expressed that very thing to her in my presence. She, of course, was **not** happy, began to put him down, shared the things they had done, and couldn't fail to mention their plans to have a future together. It was in bad taste. I told both of them they needed Jesus and that I was leaving. He did not want me to leave and, instead, asked her to leave. Although the moment wasn't pretty, it gave me some hope that he was serious "this time".

A few days go by. I had taken my daughters to New York for a few days and the day we returned, something in my spirit told me to go to his apartment. I called first, and he said he was home alone, not doing anything. I then just went over and found that she was there. ***It sent me into a frenzy!*** I had fell for his lies and cheating ways **again**! How desperate and crazy was I to believe things would be different with this man? What reason did he have to lie to me? After all, we were already divorced.

I returned home very upset and hurting deeply. I had experienced so much pain and sadness over the years. It felt as though every woman he had ever cheated with was laughing at me. He didn't respect me. He did not protect me like a husband should. And before my very eyes, he chose her over me.

I am not even sure how I made it home safely, but I did. My ex-husband called my son (who was home at the time) to tell him to make sure I was okay. I went inside and told my son I had a terrible headache. I looked in the cabinet for something to make the pain go away. The thing I needed to go away was not the headache; it was **life** I wanted to erase. I hurt so bad that even now, I cannot describe it. One thing I knew for certain: I did not want to wake up the next day feeling what I had felt the last few years before he left. Neither did I want to feel the pain of remembering the other affairs. I didn't deserve that, and even a trip to the closet could not help with this one. I was past crying and praying. I was without hope and that mustard seed of faith. Those were not pills to get rid of my headache; they were pills I thought would end my pain.

Waking up in the hospital surrounded by my mother and children, I wept as I saw them weeping and looking scared. I had hurt them and was ashamed. I woke up in even more of a mess than the night before. I had fallen below God's will because I took my eyes off of Him. The days after consisted of medication, pain, more crying, and more praying. I was moving to the other side. It was when I took my eyes off of the Lord that my feet stopped moving and the other side appeared to be an eternity away. With my natural eyes, I could not see making the journey.

CRAWL, WALK, RUN

In the darkest nights and brightest days, loneliness seemed to find me. It would lay next to me. It would be a passenger in my car, sometimes taking the back seat and whispering to my heart. It would remind me while I was watching a movie alone that it was just me. There was no one to high-five. It would talk to me on Fridays when everyone was discussing their weekend plans with their significant others and families.

Loneliness reminded me that we were 'Best Buds'. While everyone else was too busy for the company of loneliness and me, we snuggled up with our regularly-scheduled date. It made me feel used by those I loved because them excluding me meant I wasn't important to them at the time. One day, I discovered that it was not loneliness at all: It was **GOD** asking me, *"What are we doing?"*

GOD was watching the movie with me.

GOD was riding in the car with me and "came only in peace".

When I was still, He was trying to get my attention. God wanted to date me. He wanted to spend the weekend with me. He wanted to spend every moment with me.

"God, I pray you forgive me for not recognizing who you were. Forgive me for not calling on you. You said in your Word that you would never leave me nor forsake me. You, Lord, witnessed how this all went down. You saw the fight. You saw what he did. You heard what we said to each other. It was a mess! I forgot you were there, God. I'm sorry for wanting something or someone of this world more than I wanted you."

I am learning about relationships now—healthy relationships, the role I play, and the participation of others around me. I determine how I want them in my life and how much of my life they can be a part of. I draw the line and erase where lines do not belong. I am learning about my heart—why it beats, why it aches, and why I can't control the way it beats for others.

We cannot control these things alone. They are checked when we go to God and let Him know we have started to feel something that is out of our control. We need His help to check it. We need to go to God and have Him reveal to us those things that may make our heart beat but over a period of time, can cause our heart an unhealthy, extended pause.

The noise of bad relationships can ring loud and long. Sometimes, the quieter things became around me, the louder the sound of my heartbeat would be. Even the bad memories seemed to ring loudly in my ears. My dark places seemed to be filled with many people, yet it was eerily quiet. Then, when the hurt began, the heartbeats and memories flooded my soul. I sought God's peace, and I found it. I crawled, walked, and ran to His peace that passed all understanding.

THE OTHER SIDE OF THROUGH

Praise God! I made it to "The Other Side of Through!" After such a long journey, I am **rejoicing** in the victory of making it out of the dark place of depression, and although my family was broken apart, none of us were consumed in the fire. We have forgiven one another for all the hurt and harm. My ex-husband had some real struggles and strongholds, but they are **HIS TESTIMONY**—one I hope he shares with someone who may need to know his story. I have forgiven him and even commend him for doing something I could never do: *LEAVE the marriage.*

This story is not meant to show myself as a victim; nor is it meant to villainize my ex-husband. He is a good person and the father of my children. He was broken, which translated to him not being able to be a good husband for or to me. I know what it feels like to be on the run from

God or even mad at God for some crazy reason. *Be honest: We have all been there at some time in our lives.* Many of us just don't stay there—and neither did he. My ex-husband is doing well and has returned to his faith and believing in God. Since then, he's been very apologetic about the terrible things he did as a husband and for not being the best father and role model he could have been.

This story is about **ME** and **MY** struggle with rejection in a marriage, feelings of inadequacy, depression, and hopelessness. It was written in hopes that the struggles are made real enough and strong enough for someone to grab a hold of and use it as a floatation device when they are in deep, troubled waters.

Although I am healing nicely on this side, I have not forgotten about the woman who I was when I started out on this journey; the woman who married at a young age and found herself in one storm after another. I think about the woman who decided that life hurt so bad, she did not want to wake up the next morning and feel that same hurt again. It breaks my heart to know I was that woman who had so much love to give yet never loved myself. I gave away the very thing I prayed and longed for so desperately: **LOVE.**

My heart grieves for the women who may still be sitting in the dark place that I was able to leave. Let your heart be troubled not, as these words I dedicate to you and pray they are a beacon of light, just as God's words will lead you out.

Psalm 37:23 says, *"The steps of a good man are ordered by the LORD"*, so keep walking because each step you take, the Lord has ordered. They are leading you not only beside the still waters, and though you may walk through the valley of the shadow of death, always know God is there. When you least expect it, you will be standing with your shoulders squared, and chin held high—here with me on "The Other Side of Through"!

I have spent the last four years recovering from the journey. I continue to practice things like self-love and commitment to maintaining a healthy mind, body, and soul.

Healing is a process and filled with self-discovery, setbacks, emotional difficulties, laughter, and tears of joy. The bad memories are like scars not seen by the naked eye because they are behind the smiles and behind the scene, making appearances when you least expect. Still, take the time to talk through and work through each scar while being careful not to pull off the scab.

The Other Side Of Through

Traveling to "The Other Side of Through" has been quite an adventure. Before the separation, I was hurt and lonely. When he left, I was devastated, lost, hurt, and lonely. After the divorce, I was lonely, hurt, afraid, and (for the first time in years) spiritually lost. I know right from wrong. I know good from bad. Most importantly, I know the will of the Lord for my life. Now that I have "arrived", I must apply what I have learned. I must dig deep as I move forward towards building friendships and (potentially) another relationship so that I do not become bitter but better. I know God's love will cover me, even on this part of the journey, because He will let me know if the wrong man comes into my life. I must say that I have hopes of a man finding me who will think the world of me. He will look at me as though I am his 'Superwoman'…his queen. This man will laugh at the same things I laugh at, like my hilariously-corny jokes, and enjoy the simple and elegant things in life. Above all else, he will *LIKE* me.

Life has a way of showing us who we are through our relationships and friendships. I found it to be quite disheartening that I was to myself whom I let others be to me. I have heard many times before that we have to teach people how to treat us; however, they failed to mention that the teaching should be continuous. As I experienced new things and as God enlarged my territory, I became a new person. I was a new creature, slowly being disconnected from the one in which I had become one with.

Looking back, I know God must have been sad when I decided I did not want to live, all because I had placed a man upon a pedestal and deemed the love from this man so high, that the love from my Father — my **GOD** — was not enough.

The Other Side Of Through

Make notes about the path you are on. Visit them often, but do not lose your way. Maya Angelou said, *"When people show you who they are, believe them."* If I may, I would like to add, *"Pay attention because when people show you who they are, they could also be showing you who **YOU** are!"*

As people of God, especially those whom possess the gift of love, it is so very important to take note of the four-way stop signs we approach in life. Understand that if we continue straight ahead, if we are in Christ, He could easily turn that road into a dead end so that we cannot go any further. When you reach a dead end, look back and see from whence God has brought you. Understand that **HE** has been there, even when others have left us stranded and alone.

Sometimes, the journey we take is so tough that we are made stronger through the bends and winding roads. Those traveling with us may fall off, make a pit-stop, or find someone else to journey with. If we are in Christ, we understand that God is our pilot and, at times, He will take control of the flight. If we are real with ourselves, we will realize that He has always been in control…not ourselves. Typically, during stormy weather, visibility diminishes; however, in the storms of life, when you are in Christ, low visibility means that you have to fly lower than the view in which you have become accustomed to. You must adjust your eyes and heart to see through the storm. It is in the low visibility that we find ourselves before God, seeking His face and asking Him to reveal His will for our lives. God has always been concerned about our direction and journey, even when we decide to allow man to fill voids they are incapable of filling.

We pressure one another to be to us what **ONLY** God can be. We ask for people to love and cherish us without understanding what that truly means or even feels like. That in and of itself is scary because we have no gauge or measuring tool to determine if we were receiving those things we needed. We may find ourselves imagining that it would be different and, for that reason, we don't appreciate it. Instead, we sabotage it. Other instances may include when we have not asked God to show us what love is and how it feels. We fail to allow Him to first fill the voids, leaving us empty while allowing man to fill those voids with things that are temporary. When that temporary fix begins to break down, we are shattered because we took for granted the fix was permanent. We make it our foundation and begin building right away. It is upon this weak foundation that we make decisions out of emotions early on in our situations and relationships.

I wonder if there is some sort of rulebook that governs *NOT* having a rulebook. My biggest lesson learned in getting to "The Other Side of Through" was to keep breathing. Breathing is the sign of life, displayed in God's creation of Adam. God breathed into Adam, and he began to breathe. So, as you breathe, just know God has given you life. His grace and mercy are sufficient to carry you when you feel as though life has taken that same breath away.

Looking at my situations and circumstances caused me to doubt myself, as well as doubt God. Don't let people or your emotions stop you from being the best you. When you stop believing in yourself (and especially when you stop believing in God), ask God to help your unbelief.

As I reflect back, I often try to recall the moment or the event that caused me to feel paralyzed and unable to save myself. Why didn't I give myself permission to love me like I loved him? Why didn't I walk away from all that hurt me? It's strange: I blame him for my emotional trauma but never owned that I hurt me, too. I did not take care of myself. I did not respect or love myself. I treated me the same way he treated me. Why did I give him permission and control over my destiny? How did I fight for my marriage but had no desire to fight for my life? I had gotten so used to the hurt in some ways because I possessed all I needed to rid myself of it.

Weeping may endure for a night, but joy cometh in the morning! Keep praying. Keep believing in the Word of God. Keep standing firmly on His Word and always know your only option is to keep believing.

While in the hospital after attempting to take my life, I laid on the bed…wounded. My children and mom stood around me, waiting for me to wake up. I felt something hit my forearm. It was my son's tear as he held my hand, surely in prayer. I looked up and saw him. I told him not to cry. I looked to the other side and saw my daughters' eyes, also filled with tears and faces wet, looking sad because of my actions. I realized I had hurt not only myself but them as well. I spent the next few weeks recovering and resting.

One day, I woke up, stared at the ceiling, and began to see my old friends: **FAITH**, **PEACE**, and that good, old **JOY**! *"Good Morning!"* they said to me. I knew then I had made it out. They told me they were always there, alongside that **GRACE** and **MERCY** that had followed me on my journey. They said *"NO!"* to death and destruction, and ***"YES!"*** to my destiny.

There's something about walking in a bad storm when the wind is high, and the rains are hitting you in the face, which make the road hard to see. In fact, it didn't feel like I was moving at all most days until I looked up and saw that the sun was shining and the wind wasn't really wind; it was God breathing a fresh wind into my nostrils to bring me back from a dark place. The rain wasn't really rain, either; it was me drowning in my own tears.

Although I am healed, there is a scared person inside of me. Prayerfully, with the release of this book, it will bring completion to this journey. Old things are passed away and behold; all things become new.

As you can see, the journey taken to get to "The Other Side of Through" was filled with **many** emotions. The good times needed no explanation; it was those dark and lonely times I felt the need to share because those were the times when the feelings of depression and hopelessness came to visit me. Eventually, they came to live with me. I realize I invited them in, so I had to demand they go!

I am sure there are other stories out there that may be more traumatic than mine; however, the purpose and calling I had to write this book was **much** greater than me. I had to decide that guilt and shame would not stop this message from being shared. I am not what happened to me. I need to praise God because all praise, honor, and glory is due to Him who is the Author and Finisher of my faith.

I can't wait to see **YOU** on

"The Other Side of Through"!

CONCLUSION

Becoming a wife and mother at such a young age, I was unsure how I was going to make it all work. It was the church services my mom and Auntie Nae took me to, where the Word was deposited into me that was the primary source. Something in me gravitated towards the God I had heard so much about. It was also watching my brother read the Bible and kneel in prayer every night—something I needed to do as well. Given these things, I gave God a try early on in my life. I trusted Him, I trusted His Word and allowed the Holy Spirit to lead me. In trying to be a great mother and wife, I lost myself and became unsure of my purpose.

If there is any doubt or confusion about who you are, maybe starting a list of who you are **NOT** will provide more clarity. If the process of finding your purpose and what you were created to be becomes overwhelming, begin thinking about what you were **NOT** created to do. Keep working that list down and keep praying for revelation until you begin to see that *YOU* and *YOUR PURPOSE* are made known to you.

I smile as I think about how, as a child, if someone called me a name, the quick response was, *"I am not!"* Well, God wants us to do the same thing when the enemy speaks to us about who we are, how no one loves us, and how life is not worth living. God wants us to know — and I want to remind you **ALL** — that you are **NOT** defeated!

You are victorious and conquerors!

You are not *JUST* conquerors:

YOU ARE MORE THAN CONQUERORS!

ABOUT THE AUTHOR

Rosemary Hill's career started when she joined the United States Army in 1989. She initially served as a Medical Supply Specialist for three years, after which she was then trained as a Unit Supply Specialist. She deployed to Kuwait and served honorably until 2005 when she exited the military to become an Acquisition and Contracting Professional.

Rosemary Hill

Rosemary is currently the Deputy Director of Contracting, supporting various Army programs. She manages day-to-day contracting operations and evaluates program effectiveness to identify potential areas of improvement to better meet unique needs of the organization. She also provides expert acquisition and procurement advice and recommendations to the Director and other Senior Leaders within the organization on procurement and contract matters. In addition, she holds a position as the Acting Inspector General for her organization.

Rosemary holds a Level III Certification in Contracting from the Defense Acquisition University, a B.A. in Acquisition in Contracting from Strayer University, and an M.A. in Acquisition and Contracting from Webster University. She is presently preparing to take the exam to become a Certified Federal Contracts

Manager in the National Contract Management Association. She aspires to teach Contracting at the collegiate level, as well as speak to women regarding depression and overcoming life's challenges.

Rosemary is the mother of three children: Ashley, David Jr., and Amber. She takes pride in being a mother, and enjoys writing, exercising, and has a passion for supporting her family, friends, and community.

Rosemary Hill

www.ingramcontent.com/pod-product-compliance
Lightning Source LLC
Chambersburg PA
CBHW071516080526
44588CB00011B/1451